AF614132

Take My Life

By

Mark Earlix

ISBN 978-1-84728-650-5

1st Edition Printing August, 2006

Printed in the United States of America

Take My Life / Mark Earlix

Paperback, 84 Pages

Cover Design by Joseph Palazzo

1. Earlix, Mark. 2. Self. 3. Voice. 4. God--Within. 5. Healing. 6. Spirituality. 7. Peace.

Published by: The Art Of Healing Inc.

www.SpiritualMatters.us
480.423.5888

DEDICATION

For the inspiration while writing this book, thanks with deep admiration to K.C., for helping me to see a different perspective within myself and for showing me another example of being consistent, ardent and persistent in finding a way…

ACKNOWLEDGMENTS

Thanks to my friend Roy for his patience in helping transform this work into a publisher-ready format.

I also give my sincere thanks to Jeff Farias at the KPHX Studios for contributing his unique and creative expertise in helping me with the audio version of this book.

I truly want to thank Michele Heymann for seeing and acting on my vision for this book, "Take My Life;" and who as the Contributing Editor, assisted me in organizing, editing and moving this manuscript towards completion.

From my heart, I want to say thanks to Raphael for the awesomeness in Its guidance and direction, to help to fulfill my miniscule place here… In all its glorious roughness.

This book in its entirety is dedicated to God's untiring and unconditional love expressed from within and through all nonlinear and linear expressions of Its love.

Mark Earlix, 2006

Also by Mark Earlix

Creator
The Revelation of Healing Yourself and Others

Take My Life: audio CD version
Available through www.SpiritualMatters.us
And many other wonderful organizations.

Review of "Take My Life"

"This is a profound journey into the heart and soul of a mystic. *The Voice* speaks, not only to author Mark Earlix, but to each one of us… beckoning the reader to see beyond illusions of light and dark and find the truth within. Reminiscent of the masters such as Rumi, Gabrahm, Meister Eckhart and other mystics throughout the ages, *The Voice* urges us to embrace simple truth... I Am. This book will take you as deep into the mystery as you are willing to go.
Ann Albers, spiritual instructor and author. "

Take My Life is "Very poetic, esoteric and strikingly unique."

My special gift is to notice the special gifts of others and to share these impressions about the same and what I know is that...

Mark's healing gift is finding its way into more people's lives through the multiple vehicles he generates. ***Elizabeth Solomon***

In my beginnings of knowing You,
There is joy in my life.

TABLE OF CONTENTS

INTRODUCTION

The purpose of this book is to assist the path of Self-Realization, as part of the process of understanding and getting to know your Self. In this case, the communication occurs through a conversation with the "Voice" and me

I suggest that you read the entire text. Then contemplate on a stanza from a chapter each day for insight and revelation. Journaling pages are embedded throughout the book. Utilize them to relate your revelations resulting from this daily meditation.

You will notice that throughout the book, certain phrases and sentences are in **bold** font and others are in regular (not bold) font. When I (Mark) speak… it is **bold** and when the "Voice" speaks, it is not.

This book, "Take My Life," is also available as an audio CD, which is available through www.SpiritualMatters.us.

In the moments of awareness,
Knowing Your voice exhilarates me
To a greater freedom.

Part I

The Meeting

In The Middle Of My Life

Forward

In The Middle Of My Life

It was 4:44 in the morning and my body was tired. Energy was surging through me and in the atmosphere was a high-pitched sound that created loud ringing and a sporadic variety of tones coming from everywhere around. Even though my eyes were closed and there were no lights turned on, the room was still too bright.

My exhausted body stumbled into the small walk-in closet a few feet from the bed and, from habit, I automatically kneeled before a small table with a single candle burning. Lying next to the candle was a small card with a picture depicting the Archangel Raphael. The flame flickered and reminded me of the light that is carried within. For reprieve and communion, this small room is the sanctuary that I always long to use… to bring myself back to God, within the Mind of God, the One that creates.

For the past several weeks, I had experienced a self-conscious dilemma. I felt a massive need to finally eradicate the frustration, depression, egocentrism, loneliness, procrastination, denial and lack of self care that delineated my life.

I was feeling angry, not patient, wanting to yell at God and just hating the world around me.
After several minutes passed with growing frustration; I went back to bed to try to sleep for the three remaining hours, until it was time to get ready for that day's appointments. As my body dropped back into the bed, it began again.

I heard the Voice... As with the other times, the Voice started with many voices that were difficult to understand. It was the same Voice that was present many years before, in the writing of my first book and many times since. This voice is the same Voice that everyone has within, except that few take the time to listen to it or even know that it is there... Inside. The conversation is always available to me when I am willing to listen.

I yearned to be able to understand and relate, so I once again requested that the guidance and direction coming forth from within would remain and flow through One Voice, which
initially sounded as if several radios were in front of me and were tuned clearly into the same station.

That night the dilemma that started several weeks earlier, was beginning to form into an ongoing conversation. This time, imbued with a more impressive understanding, the conversation helped me to re-remember that we live in a mirror, reflective world. Knowing that what I see in others is a reflection in what I also see in myself. If this writing is applicable to me, it is also applicable for others...

Sometimes the words spoken would make perfect sense as they were shown in a knowing ethereal picturesque way in my mind… The numinous intangible pictures transferred and trickled; forming words with identifications that were sometimes difficult to understand and at times identified with nothing.

The pictures tried to form a dance within my mind, where in spite of my yearning, were not quite being able to take that next step into comprehension. Some words were incomprehensible in this realm of linearity. They spoke to another layer of consciousness, parallel and a part of this one, but without an embraceable path of entry.

Nightly, as the writing grew in length, and every morning while going over the information from the night before, a different title would come to mind.

Daily the title changed as the conversation with the Voice ensued for several weeks.

The dialog as it was expressed has a spiritual-allegorical meaning to its understanding. It remains unchanged except for those few words that I was not able to relate to or explain.

This dialog will take you to where you want to be. I invite you to go there wholeheartedly and saturate yourself, as you enjoy this experience with me.

Becoming no different than a fine thread,
Through the eye of a needle
Slipping loosely and seamlessly…
With freedom to be you,

As you step and transcend
Through the threshold.

Tell Me when.

Chapter 1

The Mirror

I Am,
Coming Forth.

I Am the peace,
The fluid truth within you,
That melds into every cell of your being
And remembers its essence.

I am that which flows forth in rhythmic streams of vibration within and forth from you.
Through every word, action and thought,
I Am.

I am present within you and continually with you,
To touch you,
For life.

I am your conscious gift,
As always,
As you accept Me...
As I always do you.

It is like having your deepest love
Coming to dinner as your guest.
To feel and know the excitement
And anticipation in your heart.

From your deepest desire,
Having made a special dinner,
In love.
You then ask deeply inside;
"Did they really enjoy it?"

To truly know Me without fear
Is as rare in the time that we encounter another for the first time.
Feeling the flutterings of the heart
And your body flushing with excitement
And knowing for that one moment in time,
Knowing that you would enjoy
Spending the remainder of your life with them...
As you know inside… that you would.

I lightheartedly open more to you,
As you consciously come to Me.
Allowing Me to touch
Every cell in your being.

To remind you of the binding force of its Being,
In truth,
To the realities of creativity
And then through the Holier Spirit of life...
It is not possible to experience anything
But Its binding love.

To be created in Its image is to be
And is re-creative in Its image.
To re-create in Its image
Is to be a co-creator.

In realizing this is you,
Is being the countless lives of rebirth.

In you, is life replicating
That which we are of.

JOURNALING

To fulfill the will of our Creator
As we learn to fulfill our own will be done...

Though awkward,
But yet still primal and drowsy awakenings....
As a child.

Chapter 2

Dilemma

"I have a dilemma, help me."

God is not mad at you.
You just think It is.
And you act out that which you think is.

Letting out the love,
Which is in your true expression...
This is what you long for.

Allowing the peace to fill you,
In its stillness,
Is there and here… waiting.

This dilemmic experience is needed to find Me.

JOURNALING

Chapter 3

Drama

"Do I create the dilemma of my dramas and traumas?"

Life is what we think life is,
To think and act is using free will,
To use as you do freely will.

"Then as I weave my story at any moment, am I barely awake?"

Before the moments of defense,
There is no cognition of awareness.
To be awakened is also your choice,
And happens as awareness startles you,
During the acts of love or fear.

JOURNALING

Chapter 4

Unconscious Choice

"I am angry at the unconscious choices I've made."

As you are truly conscious,
There is no madness,
Just awareness in peace,
There is neither judgment nor condemnation…
And no fear.

The fear, the sleep, the condemnation
And the judgment will always be
In the world…
But these transform
So that you will not have an insatiable need
To live in them predominately… or at all.
Tell Me when.

You are and have chosen a wondrous revelation
and path for life.
And as with all paths,
This path ultimately leads to Me.
Tell Me when.

JOURNALING

Chapter 5

Sabotage

"Again, it is in the thinking that I sabotage or negate myself. For less than a moment, the truth is experienced and then as a child, I react, to think and weave a story behind it."

Even the earthworm knows
How to move, burrow and replicate...
This is instinctual.

You are greater than an earthworm.
You have free will to make choices.
What choices have you made
During your moments of wakefulness?

JOURNALING

Chapter 6

The Escape

"I had put away my creativity for others attention.

I wanted to show others that I could love… as you love me."

All pain you feel within,
Is leading you deeper within Me.

You have never really lost Me.
This is your way.
I am your truth.
I am in all ways saved for a future look.

Remember the times that you found
And used others to try to hide from Me?

Remember the times that you began to ponder
And contemplate Me…
And then something remaining
Of importance to do,
Came to mind instead?

JOURNALING

Chapter 7

On The Path

"Afterwards that was my time to be; and see myself as guilty, sad and angry.

That was the time that I separated myself from God and denied the uplifting moments as they quickly ended. I was not letting the love from myself express. I froze in being me."

Each of these times was the time that
We chose,
To begin your path,
That would bring you back to Me.
To know My calling to you.

You are mad at Me.
You lash out in frustration,
By wanting something greater within.
All humanity goes through this.
Time after time,
This is the way you choose to find Me.
And now you can find Me.

JOURNALING

Chapter 8

Find Me

"God, help me to find my Self for your companionship..."

Isn't this also your prayer in finding your peace?

For those that you like and find friendship with,
This is easy for you.
And you can find those to have friendship with…
At any time,
And to also love.

For those that avoid you because of your wit or roughness or defense or candor...
This is most important that you find their friendship.
Then you know you have fulfilled something.
Find Me.

JOURNALING

Chapter 9

Guide Me

"Then Guide me to the vigilant recognition of you."

I speak for the both of us,
Are you a reflection of what I wear?
Or am I speaking of you and Me?

As you try to deny or cover yourself
With the weave of guilt…
To live and thrash in silent agony and frustration.

Think of Me when you work, play and ponder.
Imagine Me with you.
Imagine as if I were playing this game with you.

JOURNALING

Chapter 10

Identify

Humanity sees in pictures.
To know is to hear, feel, see and taste in pictures,
For a few moments, try not to.

“But this is how we identify with each other.”

This is how we commune and identify.
This is how you can find the Godliness within,
Not only for yourself,
But as you also do for others.
This is how you can identify with Me,
The God-Self within.

JOURNALING

Chapter 11

The Conscious Mind

"I love the conscious mind as I also love you, the world within."

This is not incorrect
They both are of me.

So why is there guilt?
You are my child,
I will love you as I always have.

You have My kiss of life,
Know it as you walk.
Be it,
In its obviousness and splendor.

JOURNALING

Chapter 12

Prayer

"What is the purpose of prayer?"

Prayer is recognition and acknowledgment
Of the Godliness that dwells within...
As you find the communion,
You become the communion.

As a flow of life permeates through you...
You are the living prayer in motion.
As you are the motion,
Prayer then follows you.
As all things of consciousness in fluid realms
And dimensions longed for…
The free will comes forth.

All forms of life cannot participate
In life's choices.
You have free will and you are willingly
Finding this out in your life's choices.

To knowingly choose your path at any moment in life…
Is the difference in the way you are living now.

In the Way to Me,
You can take on
And claim the true inheritance…
Then to practice and
Realize My will without resistance.

You are the living motion
Of a single continuous living event,
Realizing there is no beginning
And there is no end.

At the beginning moment of the original word…
In constant reverberation,
This continually affects all that is
And leading into every next moment that we participate in God's
Re-creation.

As you are a living organism,
So am I.
As I am,
You are learning to be.

Contemplate this,
Prayer is our unifying source.

A cord that we have connected with each other…
Its fabric enmeshed within us.
And then is the Way within.

JOURNALING

Chapter 13

The Game

God is Blue...
Your favorite Blue.
How does it feel?
With closed eyes,
Contemplate.

I will tell you what we can do,
Let's play a game called…
Find Me

Close your eyes and contemplate this:

Tell me how I fit in you.
Tell me how I feel in you.

Tell me how I sound to you…
As the living word that comes forth.
Tell me how that sounds...
Sounds through you.

Tell me how I see through you,
And with closed eyes
Stretch the muscles of your imagination.

As you play it often from within,
And know what It is,
Know that I am in your heart,
And in every particle of your being,
And every space within.

Reflect back,
How long have you been playing your other game?
Can you remember when you started?
Find the time that made you sad or mad.

Remember those times
That you had loved Me,
And the times that you had felt my love for you.
Then play my game…
Find Me.

Pray, Meditate and Contemplate
I have given you the answer to your life,
To be whole.

As you participate in life at any time.
Enjoy life…
Then you are enjoying Me.
Love life…
Then you find your love for Me.

JOURNALING

Chapter 14

The Sun And The Moon

"Does wisdom within the Light touch me?"

That touches others that they too might glimmer...
The ones that don't remember.

By the day, we are fed with the Light and Life and
Love of the Living Son/Sun.
And all of His aspects.

The moon has her cycles too,
And her qualities.

In the nighttime and as you sleep,
You are fed by the vapors of the moon…
The binding substance of the feminine
That makes you whole...
By touching you.

JOURNALING

Chapter 15

Glimpses Of Recognition

Take My consciousness outward into Spirit,
And the ethers substance that it moves through.
Through Me.

Listen all around.
Listen!
This is the answer to your prayer of
Hearing and seeing most expediently.

JOURNALING

Chapter 16

The Fire Within

Everyone knows love,
Even in the moments
Of conception…
In loves expression.

Love carries the embodiment of
The Godliness within…
Love is what you are attracted
And attached to.

Love carries and ignites the Light within you.

<u>JOURNALING</u>

In Your breezeless breath,
The expression of Your voice
Expands and moves through me.

Part 2

EXERCISES

Exercise 1

Learning To Focus, See And Manifest

In the evening, read the paragraph that you are going to contemplate the next morning.

In the nighttime before going to bed, prepare the next day's wakeful contemplation. Each morning, awaken with the intent of the day's contemplation in your memory and then re-read it.

And for the complete day, allow the thoughts that come to you to flow freely within the meaning of the words as you wash dishes, drive to work or recreate. As I will, knowing that you will too.

The contemplation of this dialog can disperse the separation that is deeply hidden within.
Your mind and your heart will transform and conform to a greater understanding of the Godliness within.

JOURNALING

Exercise 2

The Sun Within

See the Sun as the source of all life,
With rays emanating and connecting to feet,
umbilicus, hands, heart, mouth, ears, eyes
And crown.
As your source of life.

"Giving Light to ignite my life.
Then I too am a Son/sun within...
That also glistens forth to give Light."

JOURNALING

Exercise 3

Re-Creation Exercise To Manifest

"The magic mirror is used to create something and is the ability to recreate in the image of God... the things we choose in life."

Choose something in advance to manifest.
Set aside time to be alone for this exercise.
Light a candle in a private and quiet area. After you light the candle extend your arms and hands up and out from you.

Then say this invocation:

"God prepare my body and my mind, prepare me to give the most precious thing I have, me. Help me to give all I have to you so that you may freely accept all of me. That my actions might manifest freely and even more fulfilled then in my most humbled thought."

With only your deepest desire, give your prayer to God to take. And with your dominant hand extended... imagine as you draw out a magic mirror in front of you.

What is in your mind? Predetermine in desire what you are going to manifest in the mirror. Imagine it, in its completeness, so that you will not change it.

Picture it in the mirror of your mind and in front of you. See it in the mirror. Visualize the image completely fulfilled inside the mirror.

Use your finger to create a triangle, starting at the top point drawing it in the mirror. At the very top is the God point. With your finger draw down to the right to the second point which represents the Sun/Son, which is the mediator between Earth and the mind of God.

After you have this in your mind, continue your finger to the left creating the base of the triangle. The point on the left represents the feminine principle of the Spirit.

The Spirit is the life of all things, including prayers of thought... Regardless, it is your intent and will.

Then, bring this point on the left side back up to the God point on the top. This is where you give it back to God from your intent, your will to be made manifest through desire.

The image in the mirror can then be seen as gone. This is where God accepts our intent… and then it is God's, not ours any longer. This is the seed you plant for re-creation in the mind of God.

It is done,
Thy will be done.

This image is no longer yours to think of... Unless at some point you hesitate and choose not to give it all to God. If this is the case, you can start over if you choose.

JOURNALING

Part 3

Afterwards

Many months have passed since the Voice again became more audible… as I now retrieve the writings and reflect back. The Voice desires me to recognize my Self, It always exists as proof that I am not separate from my Self nor have I ever been.

The confusion and dilemma that encroached upon me… just as a blanket might cover and slowly cut off the breath of life, these have partially lifted and something greater is continually unfolding.

The inner teaching is the guidance that humanity receives.
"God is alive and well within".

Only in decadence, desolation and deprivation is there reason to see things in thc way that I am willing it to be.

The will is fulfilling the need to complete the desire for re-creation in the mind of God.

I have a choice, a potential to be and know that I allow life to freely move and live through me, as I become clearer to brighten from within.

God understands that I falter. It is not concerned with these moments... Nor does God take anything away from me. I do that, in the fear and lack of fire to be whole.

Every word, every thought and every action is living prayer.

“Help me to see.”

I am.

Also published by Mark Earlix:

Creator: The Revelation of Healing Yourself and Others. 2nd ed. A guide to understanding for healers. Over 39,000 copies sold world-wide. Paperback.

Meditation and Spiritual Exercise Audio CD'S:

1. Higher Self... A guided meditation for revelation. In sacred writings, Self is often referred to as "the small still Voice within". Through this instructive meditation you can actually learn to experience the Divine Self within you.

2. The Flow Of Life... Contemplation through imagery. This is an exercise designed to help the listener to achieve emotional, biological and physical health. Being mystical in nature, it is also designed to help the listener to achieve spiritual focus and spiritual well being.

3. Music Of The Spheres... OM has long been considered the mystical sound of Universal Creation. In *Music of the Spheres* Mark has recreated an "OM" (Aum) meditation in mystical waves and harmonious tones that blend together to create a blissful state in the listener. This OM meditation will greatly enhance your divine inward journey.

4. Light Consciousness... A peaceful imagery that leads into a spiritual awareness exercise, partially designed by one of Mark's teachers over 30 years ago. *Light Consciousness* guides you into developing your projected consciousness.

5. Orange Focus Exercise... A flow of imagery that is based on an ancient practice and one of the most powerful and productive exercises to enhance your ability to focus, utilizing the fruit of an orange.

www.ingramcontent.com/pod-product-compliance
Ingram Content Group UK Ltd.
Pitfield, Milton Keynes, MK11 3LW, UK
UKHW041923190726
13854UKWH00003B/1412